SALMON

For my father John Clark and Grandpa Clark who fished together on the Tay

First published in
the USA in 2001 by
Ryland Peters & Small, Inc.
519 Broadway, 5th Floor
New York, NY 10012

www.rylandpeters.com

10 9 8 7 6 5 4 3 2 1

Printed and bound in China

Library of Congress Cataloging-in-Publication Data
Clark, Maxine.
Salmon / by Maxine Clark ;
photography by William Lingwood.
p. cm.
Includes index.
ISBN 1-84172-187-5
1. Cookery (Salmon) 2. Salmon. I. Title.
TX748.S24 C53 2001
641.6'92--dc21
2001019410

ACKNOWLEDGMENTS
Thanks to Keracher of Whitefriars Street, Perth, Scotland, Phil Diamond of Covent Garden Fishmongers in Chiswick, and Steve Hatt of Essex Road, London for supplying the most beautiful fish.

NOTES
All spoon measurements are level unless otherwise noted.

Ovens should be preheated to the specified temperature. If using a convection oven, cooking times should be reduced according to the manufacturer's instructions. Uncooked or partially cooked eggs should not be served to the very old or frail, the very young, or to pregnant women.

DESIGNER Sailesh Patel
SENIOR DESIGNER Louise Leffler
COMMISSIONING EDITOR Elsa Petersen-Schepelern
PRODUCTION Patricia Harrington
ART DIRECTOR Gabriella Le Grazie
PUBLISHING DIRECTOR Alison Starling

FOOD STYLIST Maxine Clark
AUTHOR'S ASSISTANT Jaqueline Malouf
STYLIST Wei Tang
PHOTOGRAPHER'S ASSISTANT Emma Bentham-Wood

CONTENTS

SALMON TALES 6

LIGHT AND AIRY 8

SUPER APPETIZERS 18

PANCAKES, OMELETS, AND TARTS 26

RICE AND PASTA 36

ENTRÉES 42

INDEX 64

salmon tales

I was born beside the River Tay, one of the legendary salmon rivers in Scotland, and the river has always been a part of my life. My father and grandfather were both great fishermen, landing salmon, sea trout, and trout from the Tay and the lochs of Perthshire. But if the men in my family were good at catching fish, the women have always been brilliant at cooking them, and many of the recipes in this book have been inspired by my mother and sister.

All salmon aficionados prefer the flavor and texture of wild salmon, which was once plentiful. However it is becoming rarer and rarer, due to over-fishing and pollution. This is very sad, as the flavor and texture is so different from the farmed stock. The majority of salmon in our fish stores is farmed.

Remember that intensity of color in a salmon isn't an indicator of intensity of flavor, more of the variety. The Chinook or king salmon, which ranges from very pale to bright red, is regarded as the finest, while other varieties include coho, sockeye, pink, chum, and the Atlantic salmon.

Salmon was originally smoked as a way of preserving the fish. Nowadays, there are two ways of doing this commercially. The first and most popular is brining or salting then cold-smoking, so the flavor and perfume of the smoke permeates the flesh, but does not cook it.

Hot smoking (or kiln-roasting) cooks the flesh and imparts a smoked flavor. You can do this at home with my method for tea-smoking salmon in a wok (page 44), which is really just the same as hot-smoking.

The salmon really is the king of fish. It looks splendid, tastes marvelous and—being an oily fish—it has health benefits too! Try the recipes in this book: some I grew up with, while others I have picked up in my travels. All reflect the versatility and great taste of this magnificent fish.

light and airy

This sushi isn't so difficult to make—using the best smoked salmon cuts out the need to have absolutely fresh fish and years of sushi-chef training. It may not be truly authentic but it is perfect served with drinks on a hot summer's night.

SMOKED SALMON AND CUCUMBER SUSHI

2 cups Japanese sushi rice

2 tablespoons sugar

1 teaspoon salt

¼ cup Japanese rice vinegar

1 large cucumber, unwaxed if possible, otherwise peeled

5 sheets dried nori seaweed

8 oz. sliced smoked salmon

3 teaspoons wasabi paste

to serve

pickled ginger

Japanese soy sauce

wasabi paste

SERVES 6

Put the rice into a strainer and wash well under running water until the water runs clear. Drain well and tip into a saucepan. Add 2¼ cups water, bring to a boil, turn down the heat, and cook slowly for 10 minutes. Meanwhile, mix the sugar, salt, and vinegar in a bowl until dissolved. Tip the rice into a bowl and stir in the vinegar mixture. Spread the rice up the sides of the bowl so it will cool quickly.

Cut the cucumber into long strips, the length of the long side of the nori.

To make the sushi rolls, put a sheet of nori, shiny side down, on a sushi mat or clean cloth. Take one-fifth of the rice and spread it over the nori, leaving a clear strip down one long edge. Cover the rice with a thin layer of smoked salmon and spread with a little wasabi paste (thin it with a little water if you like). Put a cucumber stick along the side opposite the clear strip of nori. Dampen the clear end. Using the mat to help you and starting from the cucumber end, roll up like a jelly roll, sealing it into a secure cylinder with the dampened edge.

Using a very sharp knife, cut into 1-inch lengths. Repeat with the remaining seaweed, rice, and salmon.

Serve with pickled ginger, soy sauce, and more wasabi for dipping.

ASIAN

SALMON ASPICS

Serve these aspics at room temperature so they are really wobbly: there's no need to turn them out if they are set in pretty glass dishes. A lovely summer starter.

aspic

2¼ cups fish stock (page 36)

1 stalk lemongrass, halved lengthwise and chopped

3 slices fresh ginger

1 garlic clove, sliced

1 red chile, sliced

2 teaspoons Thai fish sauce

finely grated rind and juice of 1 lime

1 oz. gelatin (4 leaves or 6 level teaspoons powdered)

salmon filling

6 fresh shiitake mushrooms, finely sliced

1 ripe avocado, halved, seeded, and coarsely chopped

12 oz. cooked fresh salmon fillet, flaked into large flakes

3 tablespoons chopped fresh cilantro

6 timbale molds, ½ cup each

a baking tray

SERVES 6

To make the aspic, put all the aspic ingredients except the gelatin in a saucepan and bring slowly to a boil. Reduce the heat and simmer for 20 minutes. Cool, then pass the liquid first through a strainer, then through a paper coffee filter to catch any bits.

Pour ⅔ cup of the stock into a clean saucepan and add the shiitake mushrooms. Bring to a boil, poach for 5 minutes, then lift out the mushrooms and set aside. Sprinkle the gelatin onto the remaining liquid, let swell for 5 minutes, then melt over a gentle heat.

Stir the gelatin mixture into the remaining cold stock, taste, and season well. Mix the chopped avocado with the salmon, mushrooms, and chopped cilantro. Put the timbale molds on a baking tray, then gently spoon in the mixture. Carefully pour enough liquid into each mold to cover the salmon mixture completely. Chill for 1–2 hours until set.

To serve, dip each mold into barely warm water, count to 10, then invert them onto individual plates. (Refrigerate until ready to eat.)

Saltimbocca is usually made from thinly cut slices of veal, sage leaves, and prosciutto: using fresh salmon, it's equally delicious, elegant, and easy to make.

SALMON SALTIMBOCCA

14 oz. piece fresh salmon fillet, skin on

2 oz. prosciutto or serrano ham

fresh sage leaves

4 tablespoons unsalted butter

3 oz. mozzarella cheese, thinly sliced

salt and freshly ground black pepper

SERVES 4

Using a very sharp smoked salmon or ham knife, cut thin escalopes from the salmon in diagonal slices towards the skin.

Cut the prosciutto into similarly sized pieces and put 1 piece on each escalope. Top with a sage leaf, secure with a toothpick, and season well.

Melt the butter in a skillet and, when it stops foaming, cook the escalopes, sage-side up, for about 1 minute. Top each with a slice of mozzarella and cover the skillet. Turn the heat up and cook for 1 minute until the mozzarella has melted. Alternatively, cook under a hot broiler.

Grind over some black pepper and eat immediately while cooking the next batch.

This carpaccio, as with the more common beef version, relies on using the best and freshest raw produce. You could ask your fishmonger to slice it for you—otherwise, half-freeze it first to make cutting easier.

SALMON CARPACCIO

WITH SALSA VERDE

1 lb. fresh, firm salmon fillet, skin on

2 lemons, halved, to serve

salsa verde

2 garlic cloves, finely chopped

4 anchovy fillets in oil, rinsed

3 tablespoons chopped fresh parsley

3 tablespoons chopped fresh mint

3 tablespoons chopped fresh basil

2 tablespoons salted capers, rinsed and chopped

⅔ cup really good extra virgin olive oil

2 tablespoons freshly squeezed lemon juice

salt and freshly ground black pepper

SERVES 4

To make the salsa verde, use a mortar and pestle to crush the garlic with 1 teaspoon salt, pounding until creamy. Stir in the remaining salsa ingredients and season with pepper. Transfer to a jar and pour a layer of olive oil on top to exclude the air. This will keep for up to 1 week in the refrigerator.

Using tweezers, remove any small pin bones from along the side of salmon. Wrap the fillet in plastic and put in the freezer for 20 minutes or until just beginning to freeze.

Take a very sharp, thin-bladed knife and slice horizontally into long thin slices (part-freezing makes slicing easier).

Arrange the slices in a single layer over chilled plates and spoon over the salsa verde. Serve immediately with the halved lemons.

CLASSIC

SWEDISH GRAVLAX

Gravlax is a classic Swedish dish of raw marinated salmon flavored with dill. In pre-refrigerator days, the salmon package would be buried in the cold ground to mature. These days, it is fashionable to cure gravlax for a shorter time, but I think it gains more flavor and a firmer texture if left for 48 hours.

2 fillets fresh salmon, 1 lb. each, skin on

¼ cup sugar

⅓ cup kosher salt

2 tablespoons black peppercorns, crushed

1 large bunch of fresh dill

gravlaxsas (gravlax sauce)

¼ cup German mustard

1 teaspoon dried English mustard

3 tablespoons superfine sugar

2 tablespoons white wine vinegar

3 tablespoons sunflower oil

3 tablespoons light olive oil

3 tablespoons chopped fresh dill

SERVES 12

Using tweezers, remove any remaining bones from the salmon, then put 1 fillet, skin side down, on a large, double sheet of plastic wrap. Mix the sugar, salt, and crushed peppercorns in a bowl, then spread evenly over the flesh. Sprinkle the dill over the top. Arrange the other fillet on top to form a sandwich and wrap up tightly in the plastic. Transfer to a non-metal dish and put a small tray and a 1 lb. weight on top (I use a food can). Refrigerate for 48 hours, turning over every 12 hours. The salmon will then be ready to eat, but the longer it sits in the marinade, the stronger the flavor will be.

To make the *Gravlaxsas*, mix the mustards, sugar, and vinegar in a bowl. Slowly beat in the oils as if making mayonnaise, until the sauce is thick. Stir in the dill and refrigerate until needed (you may need to beat it again before serving).

Unwrap the fish, reserving the juices, and scrape off the excess peppercorns and herbs. Slice the salmon vertically towards the skin, about ¼ inch thick, then slice close to the skin horizontally to release the slice. Serve with the *Gravlaxsas*.

Note: Gravlax keeps well wrapped in the refrigerator. Slice the salmon as you need it, keeping it with the juices and tightly wrapping after each use. Foil tends to pit with the corrosive salt, so use plastic wrap.

VARIATION: and Juniper Pickled Salmon Finely grate the rind of 2 lemons and put in a bowl with 20 crushed juniper berries, 2 tablespoons sugar, ⅓ cup crushed kosher salt, 2 tablespoons white peppercorns, crushed, and about ½ cup gin. Wrap and chill as in the main recipe. To serve, mix 2 tablespoons horseradish sauce or creamed horseradish with the grated rind of 1 lemon. Slice the fish as in the previous recipe and serve on thinly sliced rye bread or pumpernickel with the sauce.

super appetizers

SALMON RILLETTES

Rillettes is a traditional French dish that usually features shredded pork or duck, but salmon and other oily fish make a delicious substitute in this and other pâté-style dishes. A perfect, hassle-free starter or topping for party canapés.

1 lb. salmon fillet, skin on

2½ cups fish stock (page 36)

3 fresh or dried bay leaves

3½ sticks unsalted butter, softened

12 oz. smoked salmon, unsliced and cut into chunks

1 tablespoon green peppercorns, crushed

salt, preferably sea salt

oven-baked toast, to serve

6 small pâté pots or ramekins

SERVES 6

Put the fish, skin side up, in a wide saucepan just big enough to fit. Cover with the fish stock. Add the bay leaves, heat to simmering, then poach the fish for 7 minutes. Remove from the heat and let cool in the liquid. Remove from the liquid and peel off the skin.

Melt 3 tablespoons of the butter in a skillet, add the smoked salmon, and sauté until just opaque. Cool completely.

Using a fork, shred both salmons together. Put the remaining butter in a bowl and beat with an electric beater or wooden spoon until very soft (having the butter at room temperature makes this easier). Add the salmon and peppercorns and beat together. Taste and season well. Press the mixture into the 6 small pots, level the tops with the back of a knife, then refrigerate until set and firm.

Remove from the refrigerator 15 minutes before serving so the pâté can return to room temperature, then serve with oven-baked toast.

CREAM OF SALMON SOUP

WITH CRISP SALMON CRACKLING

Salmon soup must be the epitome of luxury: add cream and it's utterly indulgent. Amazingly, roasted salmon skin, like pork skin, makes a marvelously delicious, crisp and crunchy version of crackling (but purely optional, I assure you).

4 cups fish stock (page 36)

¾ cup mixed vegetable juice, such as V8

1 garlic clove, crushed

4 bay leaves, fresh or dry

1 tablespoon sweet paprika

1 tablespoon fennel seeds

thinly peeled rind and juice of 1 lemon

12 oz. salmon fillet, skin on

¼ cup dry sherry

⅓ cup heavy cream

¼ cup freshly grated Parmesan cheese, to serve

a nonstick baking sheet

SERVES 4–6

Put the fish stock, vegetable juice, garlic, bay leaves, paprika, fennel seeds, and lemon rind in a saucepan. Add the salmon and bring to a boil. Immediately remove from the heat and let cool. Lift the salmon out of the pan onto a plate and remove the skin.

Put the salmon flesh in a blender. Strain the stock and pour about 1½ cups over the salmon. Blend until absolutely smooth. Pour into the rinsed out pan and stir in the remaining stock and lemon juice to taste. Bring to a boil and simmer for about 10 minutes to reduce a little. Stir in the sherry and cream, then taste and adjust the seasoning. Serve hot with crisp salmon crackling and grated Parmesan.

SALMON CRACKLING

For a delicious, crisp, crunchy topping, scale the salmon and remove the skin before making the soup. Stretch the skin out flat on a wooden board, then cut the skin into thin strips using a sharp knife. Arrange on an oiled baking sheet and cook in a preheated oven at 375°F for about 15 minutes or until it is very crisp and crunchy.

A mousseline is a mousse of fish, shellfish, or poultry lightened with cream and egg whites. When made with salmon, it is the most beautiful, elegant, golden-pink. It is amazingly easy to prepare too, with a spectacular effect that makes a luxurious appetizer or posh picnic dish.

SMOKED AND FRESH SALMON TERRINE

8 oz. skinless salmon fillet, cut into chunks

1 teaspoon finely grated orange zest

2 teaspoons orange juice

¼ cup chopped fresh dill or chervil

freshly ground white pepper

14 oz. smoked salmon

2 egg whites, chilled

⅔ cup heavy cream, chilled

red salad leaves, to serve

hazelnut dressing

3 tablespoons olive oil

1 tablespoon hazelnut oil

½ tablespoon lemon juice

2 tablespoons chopped hazelnuts

2 tablespoons chopped fresh parsley

salt and freshly ground black pepper

4-cup terrine mold, lightly oiled and base-lined with wax paper

SERVES 6

Put the chunks of fresh salmon into a food processor with the orange zest, orange juice, dill or chervil, and plenty of pepper. Blend until smooth. Remove the bowl from the food processor, cover, and chill.

Meanwhile, coarsely chop half the smoked salmon. Put the bowl back on the processor. With the machine running, add the egg whites through the tube, then the cream. Blend until thick and smooth—do not overwork or it will curdle. Scrape into a bowl and stir in the smoked salmon.

Carefully fill the prepared terrine with the mixture, packing down well. Level the surface and cover the top with buttered wax paper. Stand in a roasting pan and pour in hot water (bain marie) to come halfway up the sides. Bake in a preheated oven at 350°F for 35–40 minutes until firm.

Remove from the oven, let cool completely, then chill in the refrigerator. Loosen the edges with a thin knife and turn out onto a wooden board. Trim and tidy up the edges and pat dry. Wrap the terrine with the remaining smoked salmon, pressing down well, then transfer to a flat serving platter.

Put the salad leaves in a small bowl, beat the dressing ingredients together, then pour over the leaves and toss gently. Slice the terrine with a very sharp knife and serve with the salad.

SMOKED SALMON BRANDADE

1 lb. smoked salmon

1 cup milk mixed with 1 cup water

a sprig of thyme

1 bay leaf

8 peppercorns

1 lb. baking potatoes (russets), peeled

⅔ cup mild olive oil (or half olive oil, half peanut oil)

3 garlic cloves, crushed

2 tablespoons chopped capers

3 tablespoons chopped fresh chives

3 tablespoons chopped fresh parsley

freshly ground black pepper

extra oil, for drizzling

SERVES 6–8

Put the smoked salmon in a saucepan with the milk and water, thyme, bay leaf, and peppercorns. Bring to a boil, then remove from the heat and let cool in the liquid. Meanwhile, boil the potatoes for about 20 minutes until completely tender, then mash well. Keep them warm. Strain the milk from the salmon and reserve. Break up the salmon into flakes.

Heat the oil in a saucepan until hot enough to sizzle a piece of stale bread. Add a spoonful of fish and beat well. Keep adding the fish, spoonful by spoonful over a medium heat, beating well after each addition. Stir in the garlic, capers, chives, and parsley, then beat in the potato. Add some of the reserved cooking liquid to give a soft, creamy consistency. Season heavily with freshly ground black pepper.

Pile into a dish and drizzle with olive oil before serving.

TERIYAKI SALMON

Dark sweet teriyaki marinade is one of the great Japanese classics, and one of the best-known outside Japan. This is not a traditional recipe, but uses Japanese flavors such as green wasabi paste.

1 lb. salmon fillet, skinned and pin bones removed with tweezers

chopped red radishes, to serve

teriyaki marinade

1 teaspoon sugar

1 tablespoon mirin (Japanese sweet rice wine)

2 tablespoons soy sauce

1 tablespoon peanut oil

wasabi mayonnaise

1½ cups fresh mayonnaise

2–3 teaspoons wasabi paste or powder

8 bamboo skewers, soaked in water for 30 minutes

SERVES 4

Cut the salmon into thin strips, 1 inch long and about ¼ inch wide. Mix the marinade ingredients together, add the salmon strips, and toss well. Cover and set aside for 10 minutes.

Meanwhile mix the wasabi paste or powder into the mayonnaise. Thread the salmon onto the skewers in a zig-zag fashion. Put on an oiled pan and broil under a very high heat for 1–2 minutes on each side. Serve with the wasabi mayonnaise for dipping and a pile of radishes for crunch.

A brandade is a classic French dish made with salt cod, but it works very well with smoked salmon. It is best served warm with hot toast or with a tomato salad.

pancakes, omelets, and tarts

Blini are usually made with buckwheat flour, topped with sour cream and caviar or smoked salmon. I like them even better made with mashed potato: the result is light and particularly delicious with salty salmon and crème fraîche, the French version of sour cream.

FLUFFY POTATO PANCAKES

WITH SMOKED SALMON

1 lb. baking potatoes, such as russets

⅔ cup heavy cream or crème fraîche

3 eggs, separated

¼ cup chopped fresh chives

4 tablespoons unsalted butter

salt and freshly ground black pepper

to serve

1 lb. sliced smoked salmon

1¼ cups sour cream or crème fraîche

1 small bunch of chives, chopped

4 blini pans or 1 nonstick skillet and 4 ring molds

SERVES 4

Boil the potatoes until tender, then drain. Mash or sieve, then beat in the cream and egg yolks. Season with salt and pepper and beat in the chives.

Beat the egg whites in a bowl until stiff but not dry and fold into the potatoes.

Heat four blini pans* and add ½ tablespoon butter to each. When the butter is foaming, spoon in about 4 tablespoons of the mixture into each pan. Cook until browning and set, then flip over and cook for 1 minute more. Remove from the pans to a clean cloth and keep warm in the cloth. Repeat with the remaining butter and potato mixture.

Serve the potato pancakes topped with crinkled smoked salmon, a dollop of sour cream or crème fraîche, and some snipped chives.

*If using a nonstick skillet and 4 ring molds, drop 4 tablespoons of the mixture into each mold. Cook as above, and repeat until all the mixture has been used.

2 lb. firm potatoes, such as Yukon Gold

1¾ sticks unsalted butter

8 oz. thinly sliced smoked salmon

3 tablespoons chopped fresh dill

⅓ cup heavy cream

salt and freshly ground black pepper

SERVES 4

This gorgeous potato cake is made rather more decadent than usual, laden with butter and salmon. I find that a heavy nonstick skillet with an ovenproof handle is best.

Slice the potatoes very thinly either by hand, with a mandoline, or in a food processor. Rinse the slices in cold water and pat dry with paper towels. Divide into three.

Slowly melt the butter in a small saucepan and skim off any white residue or foam. Spoon 2 tablespoons of the butter into a heavy 8-inch nonstick skillet and keep the rest warm.

Using one third of the potatoes, arrange some of the slices over the bottom of the skillet in neat, overlapping circles. Scatter the remainder of this third over the top, seasoning as you go, and brushing with butter.

Arrange half the smoked salmon over the potatoes, sprinkle with half the dill, moisten with 3 tablespoons of the cream, and sprinkle with salt and pepper.

Arrange the second portion of potatoes over the top, brushing with butter and seasoning well as you go. Cover this with the remaining smoked salmon, sprinkle with the remaining dill, and moisten with the remaining cream. Season with salt and pepper. Arrange the remaining portion of potatoes over the salmon, brushing with butter and seasoning as before, then pour over any remaining butter.

Put the skillet over a medium heat and cook carefully for about 5 minutes or until the underside begins to turn golden brown. Test by carefully lifting up the edge with a spatula. Press the potatoes down firmly and cover with a lid or buttered kitchen foil. Bake in the oven in a preheated oven at 350°F for 40–45 minutes or until the potatoes are tender when pierced with a sharp knife and the underside is a deep golden brown.

Loosen the galette with a spatula so that it moves freely. Put a warm serving plate over the skillet and invert quickly onto the dish. Serve immediately.

SMOKED SALMON AND POTATO GALETTE

A frittata is an Italian omelet cooked slowly over low heat, with the filling stirred into the eggs or spread over the top. It is served perfectly set, never folded, and makes a terrific lunchtime snack or party food.

SALMON FRITTATA WITH POTATOES AND ASPARAGUS

8 oz. fresh asparagus, trimmed

6 oz. small new potatoes

6 eggs, preferably free-range

½ cup freshly grated Parmesan cheese

3 tablespoons chopped fresh mixed herbs, such as parsley, tarragon, and chervil

3 tablespoons butter

8 oz. fresh salmon, skinned and diced into large chunks

salt and freshly ground black pepper

SERVES 2–4

Steam the asparagus for 12 minutes, or until tender, then plunge into cold water to set the color and cool completely.

Cook the potatoes in boiling salted water for 15–20 minutes until tender. Cool and slice thickly. Drain and dry the asparagus and cut into short lengths.

Beat the eggs in a bowl with a pinch of salt, lots of pepper, and half the Parmesan cheese. Stir in the asparagus and herbs. Melt the butter in a 9-inch, heavy, nonstick skillet. When foaming, pour in the egg mixture, then scatter the salmon all over. Turn down the heat as low as possible. Cook for about 15 minutes until set, but with the top still a little runny.

Arrange the cooked sliced potato on top and sprinkle with the remaining Parmesan. Cook under a hot broiler until the cheese is lightly browned and the top is just set—it should not brown too much or it will dry out.

Slide onto a warm dish, cut into 4 wedges, then serve.

SMOKED SALMON AND CHIVE

SOUFFLÉ OMELET

⅔ cup milk

1 small onion, sliced

1 small carrot, sliced

1 clove

1 bay leaf

8 oz. smoked salmon

6 tablespoons butter

1 tablespoon all-purpose flour

3 large eggs, separated

⅓ cup sour cream

¼ cup chopped fresh chives

2 tablespoons freshly chopped parsley

2 tablespoons freshly grated Parmesan cheese

salt and freshly ground black pepper

SERVES 4 AS AN APPETIZER
OR 2 AS AN ENTRÉE

Put the milk in a saucepan, add the onion, carrot, clove, and bay leaf, heat until almost boiling, then turn off the heat and let stand for 10 minutes. Add half the smoked salmon, then simmer for 5 minutes until opaque. Remove the fish to a plate and flake with a fork. Strain and reserve the milk.

Melt half the butter in a small saucepan, stir in the flour, gradually beat in the reserved milk, and bring to a boil, stirring all the time until thickened. Remove from the heat.

Put the egg yolks and half the sour cream in a bowl, beat well, then stir into the sauce. Add salt and pepper to taste. Carefully stir in the cooked smoked salmon and the chives and parsley. Beat the egg whites in a second bowl until stiff but not dry, then fold into the sauce.

Melt the remaining butter in an omelet pan and pour in the salmon mixture. Cook over a medium heat until just beginning to set, then sprinkle with the remaining smoked salmon and spoon over the remaining sour cream. Carefully flip one half of the omelet over to cover the salmon. Scatter with Parmesan and finish off in a preheated oven at 400°F for 5 minutes. Serve immediately, straight from the pan.

This pretty herb and salmon omelet makes a perfect dish for a summer brunch—an interesting change from the usual smoked salmon and scrambled eggs.

My sister Jacks is the "Queen of Tarts" in our family—she makes THE best tarts: her pastry is sublime and this is one of her best. Pastry should be handled as little as possible or it will toughen. If you have hot hands, like me, a food processor will change your life in the pastry department.

SALMON TART

GLAZED WITH LIME HOLLANDAISE

1⅔ cups all-purpose flour

½ teaspoon salt

1 stick butter, chilled

1 egg yolk

1 tablespoon chilled water

salmon filling

2 tablespoons butter

1 shallot, finely chopped

2 tablespoons all-purpose flour

1½ cups milk

2 large egg yolks

10 oz. cooked salmon, flaked with a fork

2 tablespoons chopped fresh dill or parsley

1 teaspoon prepared horseradish

1 tablespoon lime juice

salt and freshly ground black pepper

lime hollandaise sauce

3 tablespoons white wine vinegar

3 black peppercorns

1 bay leaf

1 blade of mace or
¼ teaspoon grated nutmeg

1 large egg yolk

6 tablespoons butter

finely grated zest and juice of 1 lime

salt, preferably sea salt

1 large tart pan, 8 inches diameter,
or 6 small, 4 inches diameter

foil and baking beans or rice

SERVES 6

To make the pastry, put the flour, salt, and butter in a food processor and blend until it forms fine crumbs. Mix the egg yolk in a bowl with 1 tablespoon chilled water, add to the food processor, and blend until it just starts coming together. Tip out onto a board and knead until smooth. Form the pastry into a disk, then wrap in plastic and chill for 30 minutes.

Meanwhile, to make the filling, melt the butter in a saucepan, add the shallot, and cook until soft. Add the flour and cook for 30 seconds. Stir in the milk and bring to a boil, stirring all the time. Simmer for 2 minutes then remove from the heat and let cool.

Roll out the pastry on a floured board and use to line the pan or pans. Prick the bases with a fork and line each with a square of foil. Fill with baking beans or rice, transfer to a baking sheet, and bake in a preheated oven at 375°F for 10 minutes. Remove the foil and beans.

Beat the egg yolks into the sauce and stir in the salmon, dill or parsley, horseradish, and lime juice to taste. Season well. Spoon the filling into the tart or tarts and bake at the same temperature for 20 minutes until set (the larger one may take longer).

Meanwhile to make the hollandaise, put the vinegar, peppercorns, bay leaf, and mace into a small saucepan and bring to a boil. Boil until reduced to 1 tablespoon. Beat the egg yolk in a bowl with a pinch of salt and 1 tablespoon of the butter. Set the bowl over a saucepan of simmering water and beat until slightly thickened. Strain in the vinegar, then beat in the remaining butter bit by bit until the sauce has thickened. Stir in the lime zest and season with salt, pepper, and lime juice.

Spread the hollandaise over the tart or tarts and cook under a hot broiler just until browned. Serve warm with a spinach salad.

SMOKED SALMON
SAFFRON AND LEEK RISOTTO

Though tempting, it is not traditional to serve Parmesan with fish risotto or pasta—it is said to detract from the delicate flavor. However, it's a free world!

⅓ cup olive oil

1 lb. medium leeks, thinly sliced, well washed, rinsed, drained, and patted dry

2 garlic cloves, finely chopped

2½ cups risotto rice, such as arborio, carnaroli, or vialone nano

1¼ cups medium white wine

1 teaspoon saffron threads

about 4 cups well-flavored fish stock*

8 oz. smoked salmon, coarsely chopped

¼ cup sour cream or crème fraîche (optional)

salt and freshly ground black pepper

fried leeks

2 leeks, cut into 2-inch lengths, halved lengthwise, opened out and cut into long shreds

peanut oil, for frying

SERVES 4

Heat the olive oil in a sauté pan. Add the leeks and sauté until beginning to soften and color slightly. Stir in the garlic and cook for a few minutes more. Add the rice and stir until well coated with oil and heated through. Pour in the wine and boil over a medium heat until completely evaporated. Stir in the saffron.

Add the stock, 1 large ladle at a time, stirring until each has been absorbed by the rice. Continue until the rice is tender and creamy, but the grains still firm. Gently fold in the smoked salmon and sour cream or crème fraîche, if using. Season well, then cover and let rest for 1 minute before serving in warm bowls with a froth of fried leek on top.

To fry the leeks, half-fill a small saucepan with peanut oil and heat until a small cube of bread will brown in about 30 seconds. Add the leek and fry until brown and crisp. Remove and drain on crumpled paper towels.

***Note:** Fish stock is sold in some supermarkets and most fish stores. To make it yourself, use 3 lb. fish trimmings (the frames, heads, and skin) of non-oily fish—though you can use salmon if the stock is being used for one of these salmon recipes. Put the trimmings in a large saucepan. Add 1 chopped onion, the chopped white part of 1 small leek, 1 chopped celery stalk, 1 bay leaf, 6 parsley stalks, 10 peppercorns, and 2 cups white wine. Add 5 cups water and heat slowly to just below boiling point. Don't let it boil or it will become cloudy. Simmer gently for 20 minutes, skimming any foam from the surface. Strain through a cheesecloth-lined strainer, let cool, then refrigerate.

rice and pasta

Of course you can use store-bought fresh pasta, but it's nowhere near as good as the kind you make yourself. Try this one flavored with dill and black pepper—really punchy with rich smoky salmon and the sharpness of lemon butter sauce.

SMOKED SALMON IN LEMON CREAM SAUCE WITH DILL TAGLIATELLE

8 oz. smoked salmon

chopped fresh dill, to serve

fresh pasta

2 cups bread flour or all-purpose flour

½ teaspoon salt

3 medium eggs

1 tablespoon olive oil

1 tablespoon freshly ground black pepper (very finely ground)

1½ cups (2 oz.) fresh dill sprigs

fine semolina flour, for dusting

lemon cream sauce

peeled rind of 2 lemons

1¼ cups heavy cream

⅔ cup well-flavored fish stock (page 36)

SERVES 4

To make the pasta, sift the flour and salt onto a board and make a well in the center. Put the eggs, oil, black pepper, and dill in a food processor, blend until smooth, then pour into the flour well. Gradually mix the eggs into the flour and bring the dough together. Knead for 5–10 minutes until smooth. Wrap in plastic and let rest at room temperature for 30 minutes.

Using a pasta machine, roll the dough into sheets, then cut into tagliatelle—strips about ½ inch wide. Hang up to dry slightly or arrange on clean cloths dusted with semolina flour.

Cut the smoked salmon into strips, cover, and set aside.

To make the sauce, put the peeled lemon rind into a saucepan, add the cream and fish stock, bring to a boil, then remove from the heat to infuse for 15 minutes. Remove the lemon rind and boil rapidly until slightly thickened and reduced.

Bring a large saucepan of salted water to a boil. Throw in the tagliatelle, stirring well. Return to a boil—when the water is boiling again, the pasta is cooked. Drain well and quickly toss with the sauce and smoked salmon. Transfer to warm bowls and scatter with more chopped dill. Serve immediately.

SALMON KEDGEREE

Kedgeree is a very British breakfast dish—based on an idea brought back from India by returning old Colonial types who couldn't bear to live without the delicious flavors they'd found there. This one is very special, but not for purists.

⅔ cup mixed colored rice, such as black wild rice, red Camargue-style rice, and white basmati

about 4 tablespoons butter (you may like to add more)

about 2 cups large cherry tomatoes, halved

1 bunch of scallions, chopped

1 tablespoon Thai red curry paste

12 oz. fresh cooked salmon (or tea-smoked salmon—see page 44), skinned and flaked

a splash of vinegar

4 small very fresh eggs

3 tablespoons chopped fresh cilantro

2 large red chiles, seeded and chopped

salt and freshly ground black pepper

SERVES 4

Cook each kind of rice separately: use 3 times the volume of boiling salted water for wild and red rice, cooking the wild rice for 55–60 minutes and Camargue for about 45–60 minutes or until done. Drain well. To cook basmati rice, put it in a saucepan, add water to come ½ inch over the top of the rice. Bring to a boil, cover with a lid, reduce to the lowest possible heat, and cook for 10–12 minutes. Turn off the heat and let stand for 2 minutes, still covered.

Melt the butter in a skillet and, when the foaming has subsided, add the halved tomatoes, cut-side down. Cook over a brisk heat for 2–3 minutes without moving them, until browned, then turn them over, add the chopped scallions and cook for 1 minute. Stir in the curry paste, then the rice and the salmon. Add salt and pepper to taste, then cover and keep the mixture warm.

Bring a saucepan of water to a boil and add a splash of vinegar. Crack open each egg and slip it into the water. Return to a boil, then reduce the heat and simmer for 2 minutes. Lift out of the water with a slotted spoon and drain well on paper towels.

Uncover the kedgeree, put the eggs on top, scatter with chopped cilantro and chiles, and serve.

entrées

ONE-SIDED SALMON

WITH QUICK HOLLANDAISE

A way of cooking a salmon fillet in a skillet, skin-side down, so that it remains moist all the way through and doesn't need turning. The salmon skin will be beautifully crisp.

4 salmon fillets, 7 oz. each, cut from the middle of the fish, skin on

peanut or sunflower oil

quick hollandaise

2½ sticks unsalted butter

4 egg yolks

tarragon vinegar

freshly squeezed lemon juice, to taste

salt and freshly ground white pepper

SERVES 4

To make the hollandaise, melt the butter in a small saucepan and heat to boiling point.

Mix the egg yolks in a blender with 1 tablespoon tarragon vinegar. When the butter is boiling, carefully pour it onto the egg yolks WITH THE MACHINE RUNNING. The butter will cook and thicken the yolks giving a beautifully smooth sauce. Taste and season with more vinegar, lemon juice, and salt and pepper to taste. Keep the sauce warm in a bain marie but do not let it get too hot or it will split (curdle).

Brush the skin sides of the salmon with a little oil. Heat a skillet to medium hot. Add the salmon fillets, skin side down—DO NOT MOVE THEM. Cook over a medium heat (they should sizzle gently, not fizz or smoke) for 10 minutes—have a look, they should be cooking from the skin side upwards. Cook a little longer until the fish looks almost cooked through and opaque. NOW turn the fillets over and cook for 1 minute. The skin will be crisp and golden and completely edible, the flesh moist and delicate. Serve with the quick hollandaise.

Hot-smoke your own salmon quickly and easily with the delicate fragrance of tea in a wok (or covered outdoor grill). I've shamelessly pinched this delicious salsa from my friend, the Scottish chef Nick Nairn.

TEA-SMOKED SALMON

WITH AVOCADO SALSA

4 salmon fillets, 4 oz. each, skinned

½ cup mirin (Japanese sweet rice wine) or dry sherry

1 tablespoon sugar

1 tablespoon salt

2 tablespoons finely chopped fresh ginger

avocado salsa

1 ripe Hass avocado

2 ripe plum tomatoes, skinned, seeded, and diced

1 red onion, finely chopped

3 tablespoons chopped fresh cilantro

2 teaspoons Japanese pickled ginger, chopped

1 mild red chile, seeded and chopped

finely grated zest and juice of ½ lime

sea salt and freshly ground black pepper

smoking mixture

1 cup long-grain rice

1 cup sugar

1 cup Chinese leaf tea

1 wok or kettle

1 piece aluminum foil

1 bamboo steamer, with lid

2 wet cloths

SERVES 4

Arrange the salmon in a non-metal dish. Put the mirin, sugar, and salt in a bowl with ½ cup water, stir until dissolved, then add the ginger. Pour the mixture over the salmon, turning to coat, then cover and marinate for 1 hour in the refrigerator.

To make the salsa, halve the avocado and remove the pit. Chop the flesh into tiny dice and transfer to a small bowl. Add the tomatoes, onion, cilantro, pickled ginger, chile, lime zest and juice, salt, and pepper and mix well. Let marinate for 30 minutes and serve with the salmon.

Meanwhile, lift the salmon out of the liquid and lay it carefully in the base of the bamboo steamer and put the lid on firmly.

To smoke the fish, line a lidded wok or kettle with foil, then put the rice, sugar, and tea on top of the foil. Stir gently to mix. Heat the wok over a medium heat until the mixture starts to smolder. Put the bamboo steamer and lid on top and seal the seam between the bamboo steamer and wok with wet cloths.

Reduce the heat to low and leave to smoke for 15 minutes. Turn off the heat and let it smoke for another 15 minutes. Take the wok outside before lifting the lid. The salmon will be perfectly cooked and lightly scented with the smoke. Serve warm with the salsa.

SALMON FISHCAKES

WITH SEAWEED AND A SESAME SEED CRUST

I used to make traditional fishcakes for a gourmet store in London's Mayfair, spreading the mixture onto trays to set, cutting out shapes with a cookie cutter, then freezing. When frozen, they were much easier to egg and crumb and would keep for ages in the freezer. Try it with this more glamorous version.

1 lb. cooked fresh salmon or hot-smoked salmon

1 tablespoon Thai fish sauce

1½ cups cooked mashed potatoes (plain, with no butter or milk)

3 sheets nori seaweed, chopped or crumbled

1 teaspoon kalonji (black onion or nigella seeds) (optional)

2 teaspoons sesame oil

⅓ cup sesame seeds

⅓ cup dried unseasoned breadcrumbs

all-purpose flour, for dusting

2 eggs, beaten

peanut or corn oil, for frying

soy sauce and chile sauce, for dipping

SERVES 4–6

Remove any skin from the salmon and flake the flesh with a fork. Add the fish sauce to the potatoes, then beat until thoroughly mixed. Mix in the seaweed, kalonji (if using), and sesame oil, then fold in the salmon. Shape the mixture into 8–12 patties, flattening them slightly. Mix the sesame seeds and breadcrumbs in a bowl. Dip each fishcake in flour, then beaten egg, then the sesame crumbs. The fishcakes can now be frozen to cook at a later date.

When ready to cook, heat the oil in a deep-fryer to 350°F. Fry the fishcakes for about 5 minutes until crisp and golden, then drain well on paper towels. Serve with a little soy sauce or chile sauce for dipping.

Note: Deep-frying is the best way to cook these fishcakes: they cook evenly all over and if the oil is at the right temperature, they will not absorb it, but will be golden and crisp on the outside.

VARIATION: For classic fishcakes, substitute 2 tablespoons chopped fresh parsley for the seaweed and leave out the sesame oil and kalonji. Use 2 cups fresh or ⅔ cup dried breadcrumbs to coat. Roll into classic rounds or into croquette shapes.

1 tablespoons mixed red, green, and white dry peppercorns

4 salmon fillets, 7 oz. each, skin on

5 cups fresh wholemeal breadcrumbs

⅔ cup shelled walnuts, chopped

½ cup mixed chopped fresh herbs

finely grated zest of 1 orange

freshly grated nutmeg

1 stick butter, melted

1 egg yolk, beaten

salt and freshly ground black pepper

homemade tartare sauce

⅔ cup homemade mayonnaise (page 51)

1 tablespoon chopped capers

1 tablespoon chopped gherkins

1 tablespoon chopped fresh parsley

1 shallot, finely chopped

1 teaspoon lemon juice

salt and freshly ground black pepper

SERVES 4

Pound the peppercorns with a mortar and pestle. Rub this mixture all over the flesh side of the fillets. Put the fillets into a baking dish, skin side up.

Mix the breadcrumbs with the walnuts, herbs, orange zest, and lots of nutmeg. Melt the butter in a skillet and, when foaming, stir in the breadcrumb mixture. Cook over a high heat until the butter is absorbed and the breadcrumbs are beginning to brown. Season well with salt and freshly ground black pepper.

Brush the salmon skin with beaten egg yolk and press on the breadcrumbs. Bake in a preheated oven at 400°F for 15–20 minutes until the fish is opaque and the crumbs crisp.

Mix the tartare sauce ingredients together in a small bowl and serve with the fish.

HERB AND NUT CRUSTED SALMON FILLETS

I love to serve this dish with a pile of buttery leeks and the creamiest of mashed potatoes flavored with a honey and wholegrain mustard.

This is the classic way to poach a whole salmon, whether serving hot or cold. Ever since I can remember, my mom has served this Danish sweet and sour cucumber salad with cold poached salmon or sea trout—it is the perfect accompaniment.

COLD POACHED SALMON

WITH MAYONNAISE AND SWEET AND SOUR CUCUMBER

one 3lb. salmon

thick homemade mayonnaise, to serve (see note)

court bouillon

1 tablespoon salt

⅔ cup white wine

1 onion, sliced

2 celery stalks, sliced

1 carrot, sliced

a handful of parsley stalks

2 bay leaves

1 teaspoon black peppercorns

cucumber salad

2 large cucumbers

1 tablespoon salt

1 tablespoon sugar

½ cup white wine or cider vinegar

2 tablespoons chopped fresh dill

freshly ground white pepper

SERVES 6

To make the cucumber salad, peel the cucumbers and slice as thinly as possible with a mandoline or in a food processor. Spread in a colander and sprinkle with the salt, mixing well. Stand the colander on a plate and let drain for 30 minutes. Rinse well and squeeze the moisture out of the cucumber. Spread the cucumber over a large plate. Dissolve the sugar in the vinegar and stir in the dill. Pour over the cucumber and let marinate for at least 1 hour. Grind over lots of white pepper just before serving.

Put all the court bouillon ingredients into a large saucepan, add 6 cups water, bring to a boil, and simmer for 1 hour. Cool completely, then strain the liquid into a fish kettle. Put the salmon on the rack of the kettle and lower it into the liquid. The liquid must cover the fish—if not, top up with a little water. Bring slowly to the boil, then cover and switch off the heat. Let cool completely in the liquid.

When completely cold, lift out and drain the fish. Remove the skin, then slide the fish onto a serving dish. Serve with thick homemade mayonnaise and the cucumber salad.

If serving hot, bring it to the boil, lower the heat to a bare simmer and poach for 4 minutes per pound then remove it from the liquid, remove the skin, and serve with melted butter.

Note: To make homemade mayonnaise, put 2 egg yolks, 1 teaspoon dry mustard powder, and a pinch of salt in a small bowl. Using an electric hand beater, beat in, little by little, ⅔ cup light olive oil. When thick, add 2 tablespoons lemon juice, then beat in another ⅔ cup olive oil until thick. Season with salt and pepper.

GLAZED SALMON STEAKS WITH BASIL OIL

An updated version of an Italian method of cooking in agrodolce—meaning sweet and sour.

2 tablespoons balsamic vinegar

2 teaspoons soy sauce

4 salmon steaks, 7 oz. each

⅓ cup extra virgin olive oil

1½ cups fresh basil leaves

salt and freshly ground black pepper

extra basil leaves, to serve

SERVES 4

Mix the balsamic vinegar and soy sauce in a shallow dish, then add the salmon, turning to coat. Cover and let marinate in the refrigerator for at least 30 minutes.

Put the olive oil and basil in a blender and purée until smooth, cover, and leave to infuse. Alternatively, use a bowl and a hand blender.

Remove the salmon from the marinade (reserving the marinade) and drain well. Heat a nonstick skillet until very hot. Add the steaks and cook without moving for 3 minutes, then turn over and cook for 2 minutes on the other side. Transfer the steaks to a plate to keep warm. Deglaze the skillet with the reserved marinade, boiling until thickened and syrupy (add a little water if necessary).

Whisk the basil oil again if it has separated, then serve the steaks brushed with the reduced pan juices, drizzled with the oil, and sprinkled with extra basil leaves.

Watch the steaks carefully while cooking—they can easily overcook. Brushing the bars of the grill with a little oil will prevent the salmon from sticking. We should use flavored butters more—they are delicious!

GRILLED SALMON STEAKS

WITH BASIL AND PARMESAN BUTTER

6 fresh salmon steaks, cut about 1 inch thick, 3 lb. total weight

basil parmesan butter

1½ sticks unsalted butter

¼ cup freshly grated Parmesan cheese

1 teaspoon balsamic or sherry vinegar

¼ cup fresh basil leaves, sliced

freshly ground black pepper

marinade

1 large garlic clove, crushed

⅓ cup light olive oil

2 tablespoons balsamic or sherry vinegar

1–2 sprigs of thyme, crushed

SERVES 6

To make the basil and Parmesan butter, beat the butter with an electric mixer until soft. Gradually beat in the grated Parmesan, vinegar, basil leaves, and ground black pepper to taste. Scoop onto to a piece of wet wax paper and roll into a cylinder. Wrap in plastic and refrigerate (or freeze) for at least 1 hour, or until firm.

Put the marinade ingredients in a wide, shallow dish, mix well, then add the salmon steaks and turn to coat well. Cover and let marinate for 20–30 minutes. Lift the steaks from the marinade and pat dry with paper towels.

Heat an outdoor grill until the coals are MEDIUM hot and white (no longer red). Lightly oil the grill bars, add the salmon, and cook for about 3 minutes on each side until crisp and brown on the outside and just opaque all the way through—overcooked salmon is dry, so be careful to cook it properly. Serve the salmon steaks covered with slices of the chilled butter melting on top.

Note: If using other herbs, such as parsley, tarragon, or marjoram, always use fresh: dried herbs are not very successful.

Originally a way to cook fresh trout brought straight from river to fire, this method lends itself beautifully to cooking a whole fish so that it retains all its flavor and moisture.

SALMON BAKED IN NEWSPAPER

1 fresh salmon, about 3 lb., gutted but not scaled

1 lemon, sliced

a bunch of fresh herbs such as dill, tarragon, chervil, and bay leaves

4 sheets black and white newspaper

1 large sheet wax paper

SERVES 6

Open the newspaper sheets and arrange one on top of each other. Fill a sink with cold water and soak the newspaper in it. Wet the wax paper and open it out flat on a work surface.

Put the salmon on top of the wax paper and tuck the lemon slices and herbs into the cavity. Wrap up in the wax paper. Spread the soaked newspaper on the table and put the wrapped fish at the long edge. Roll up, tucking in the sides. Put the fish on a baking tray and bake in a preheated oven at 400°F for about 45 minutes.

Remove from the oven and unwrap. Test to see if the fish is cooked through (the eye should be white and the flesh opaque to the bone). If not done, wrap up again, spray with water, and cook for another 10 minutes and check after that.

To serve, unwrap the fish and roll onto a serving platter in all its glory. It will taste sublime.

SALMON BAKED IN A SALT CRUST

This ancient way of cooking a whole fish seals in all the juices. Lots of salt is needed, but none of it is eaten. The fish comes out fantastically moist and not at all salty.

1 whole salmon, 4 lb., unscaled but gutted through the gills if possible (ask the fishmonger to do this for you)

2 egg whites

about 4 lb. kosher or sea salt, depending on the size of the dish

oil, for brushing

SERVES 6

Choose an oval or rectangular baking dish into which the salmon will fit very comfortably without touching the edges. Lightly wipe inside the dish with oil.

Put the egg whites in a bowl with 6 tablespoons water and beat lightly. Mix in the salt with your hands as if you were rubbing in the fat when making pastry. Cover the base of the dish with a 1-inch layer of salt. Put the fish on top and cover thickly with the remaining moist salt.

Bake in a preheated oven at 375°F for about 1 hour. Remove from the oven and rest for 10 minutes.

To serve, carry to the table with full ceremony and crack the crust open (you may need a hammer). The skin may come away with the salt crust. Remove the top crust. Lift the fish off the bone, then lift out the bone. Cut through the bone at the head and remove it to reveal the remaining fish on the other side. Lift this away from the skin. Serve as quickly as possible with Quick Hollandaise (page 43) or Basil Oil (page 52): the fish should be served as plainly as possible—the flavor is very pure.

PLANKED SALMON

1 side or fillet of salmon, about 2½ lb., skin on

olive oil

2 tablespoons honey, warmed

3 tablespoons wholegrain mustard

salt and freshly ground black pepper

1 cedar plank
(if unavailable, use a baking sheet)

SERVES 4–6

Make sure the fish fits the plank and that both will fit in your oven. Brush the fish lightly with olive oil. Put the fish, skin side down, on the plank and put into a cold oven. Turn the oven on to 325°F. Bake for 20 minutes, then check the fish. It should look opaque—check that it will flake easily when a knife is inserted into the thickest part. Depending on the thickness of the salmon, it could take up to 40 minutes to cook.

Spray the salmon and plank with water from time to time to release more flavor.

Mix the honey with the mustard and spread over the salmon. Cook under a preheated broiler for 2–3 minutes until golden and glazed. Remove from the heat, let cool, and serve cold.

Cooking a side of salmon on a cedar plank was originally done by Native Americans over a wood fire—the cedar imparted a particular fragrance to the salmon. In this recipe it is baked in the oven. The salmon is then spread with honey and mustard, grilled to glaze, then served cold.

A fantastic way to roast or grill a gigot *of salmon. If you have an outdoor grill with a lid, the salmon will take a shorter time to cook—just don't keep lifting the lid.*

MUSTARD-GRILLED SALMON TAIL

2 fresh tail-end salmon fillets, 14 oz. each, skin on

salt and freshly ground black pepper

mustard marinade

3 tablespoons Dijon mustard

2 tablespoons soy sauce

1 large garlic clove, crushed

1 tablespoon chopped fresh ginger

3 tablespoons chopped fresh tarragon

thick kitchen twine, soaked in cold water

SERVES 6–8

To make the marinade, mix the mustard, soy, garlic, ginger, and tarragon in a bowl.

Put one salmon fillet skin-side down on a board and spread liberally with the mustard mix. Season well. Arrange the other fillet on top and tie up in 3 or 4 places with twine. Cover and refrigerate for about 2 hours for the flavors to permeate the flesh. Return to room temperature before cooking.

When ready to cook, preheat an outdoor grill until the coals are white and no longer red. Brush the salmon with a little oil and grill over MEDIUM hot coals for about 15 minutes per side, or until the fish is opaque all the way through.

Serve immediately by untying the twine and lifting off the top fillet. Lift the salmon off the skin to serve.

Note: There are heavy foil trays available: if you "roast" the salmon on one of these, it will catch the delicious juices.

INDEX

asparagus, salmon frittata with potatoes and, 31
aspic, asian salmon, 10
avocado, tea-smoked salmon with salsa, 44

brandade, smoked salmon, 24

carpaccio, salmon, with salsa verde, 14
classic Swedish gravlax, 16
cream of salmon soup with crackling, 20
cucumber, sushi, smoked salmon and, 8

eggs:
  salmon frittata with potatoes and asparagus, 31
  smoked salmon and chive soufflé omelet, 32

fillet:
  asian salmon aspic, 10
  cream of salmon soup with crackling, 20
  herb and nut crusted salmon fillets, 48
  one-sided salmon with quick hollandaise, 43
  salmon carpaccio with salsa verde, 14
  salmon frittata with potatoes and asparagus, 31
  salmon kedgeree, 40
  salmon rillettes, 19
  salmon saltimbocca, 13
  salmon tart glazed with lime hollandaise, 35
  smoked and fresh salmon terrine, 23
  teriyaki salmon, 24
fishcakes, salmon, with seaweed and sesame seed crust, 47
fluffy potato pancakes with smoked salmon, 27
galette, smoked salmon and potato, 28
gin and juniper pickled salmon, 17
glazed salmon steaks with basil oil, 52
gravlax, classic Swedish, 16

herbs:
  glazed salmon steaks with basil oil, 52
  grilled salmon steaks with basil and Parmesan butter, 55
  herb and nut crusted salmon fillets, 48

pancakes, fluffy potato, with smoked salmon, 27
pasta, smoked salmon in lemon cream sauce with dill tagliatelle, 39
planked salmon, 60
poached salmon, cold, with mayonnaise and sweet and sour cucumber, 50

rice:
  smoked salmon, saffron and leek risotto, 36
  salmon kedgeree, 40
rillettes, salmon, 19

salsa:
  salmon carpaccio with salsa verde, 14
  tea-smoked salmon with avocado salsa, 44
saltimbocca, salmon, 13
smoked salmon:
  fluffy potato pancakes with, 27
  smoked and fresh salmon terrine, 23
  smoked salmon and chive soufflé omelet, 32
  smoked salmon and cucumber sushi, 8
  smoked salmon and potato galette, 28
  smoked salmon brandade, 24
  smoked salmon, saffron, and leek risotto, 36
  tea-smoked salmon with avocado salsa, 44
steaks:
  barbecued, with basil and Parmesan butter, 55
  glazed, with basil oil, 52
soup, cream of salmon with crackling, 20
sushi, smoked salmon and cucumber, 8

tart, salmon, glazed with lime hollandaise, 35
tea-smoked salmon with avocado salsa, 44
teriyaki salmon, 24
terrine, smoked and fresh salmon, 23

whole salmon:
  poached salmon, cold, with mayonnaise and sweet and sour cucumber, 50
  salmon baked in newspaper, 56
  salmon baked in a salt crust, 59

conversion charts

Weights and measures have been rounded up or down slightly to make measuring easier.

VOLUME EQUIVALENTS:

American	Metric	Imperial
1 teaspoon	5 ml	
1 tablespoon	15 ml	
¼ cup	60 ml	2 fl.oz.
⅓ cup	75 ml	2½ fl.oz.
½ cup	125 ml	4 fl.oz.
⅔ cup	150 ml	5 fl.oz. (¼ pint)
¾ cup	175 ml	6 fl.oz.
1 cup	250 ml	8 fl.oz.

WEIGHT EQUIVALENTS:

Imperial	Metric
1 oz.	25 g
2 oz.	50 g
3 oz.	75 g
4 oz.	125 g
5 oz.	150 g
6 oz.	175 g
7 oz.	200 g
8 oz. (½ lb.)	250 g
9 oz.	275 g
10 oz.	300 g
11 oz.	325 g
12 oz.	375 g
13 oz.	400 g
14 oz.	425 g
15 oz.	475 g
16 oz. (1 lb.)	500 g
2 1b.	1 kg

MEASUREMENTS:

Inches	Cm
¼ inch	5 mm
½ inch	1 cm
¾ inch	1.5 cm
1 inch	2.5 cm
2 inches	5 cm
3 inches	7 cm
4 inches	10 cm
5 inches	12 cm
6 inches	15 cm
7 inches	18 cm
8 inches	20 cm
9 inches	23 cm
10 inches	25 cm
11 inches	28 cm
12 inches	30 cm

OVEN TEMPERATURES:

110°C	(225°F)	Gas ¼
120°C	(250°F)	Gas ½
140°C	(275°F)	Gas 1
150°C	(300°F)	Gas 2
160°C	(325°F)	Gas 3
180°C	(350°F)	Gas 4
190°C	(375°F)	Gas 5
200°C	(400°F)	Gas 6
220°C	(425°F)	Gas 7
230°C	(450°F)	Gas 8
240°C	(475°F)	Gas 9